This book

belongs to

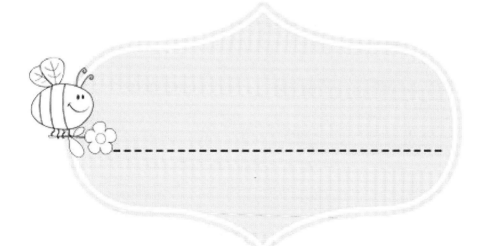

- -

English - Arabic

watermelon

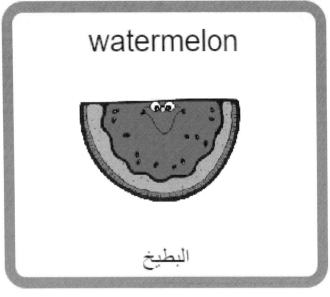

البطيخ

crab

سلطعون

water

ماء

medicine

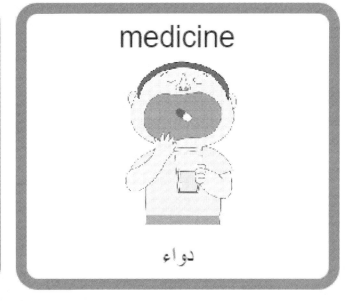

دواء

cooking

طبخ

quiz

لغز

salad

سلطة

king

ملك

rat

فأر

box

صندوق

aggressive

العدواني

jam

مربى

snowflake

ندفة الثلج

music

موسيقى

barber

حلاق

coconut

جوزة الهند

shopping

التسوق

fresh

طازج

porcupine

النيص

turnip

لفت نبات

carpenter

النجار

elephant

فيل

proud

فخور

pearls

درر

bin

بن

candy

حلويات

beg

إفترض جدلا

scary

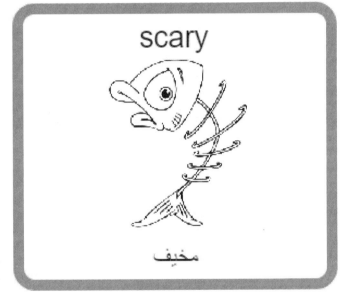

مخيف

paper

ورقة

factory

مصنع

ladder

سلم

science

علم

whale

حوت

doll

دمية

happy

السعيدة

fireplace

المدفأة

knife

سكين

van

سيارة نقل

moon

القَمر

chili

الفلفل الحار

nut

جوز

cab

سيارة أجرة

toilet

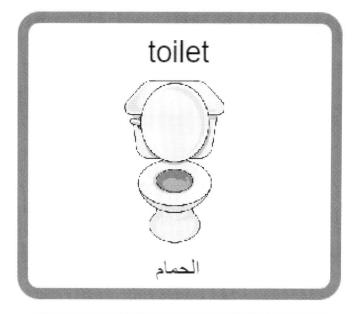

الحمام

bucket

دلو

insect

حشرة

tiger

نمر

shy

خجول

vegetable

خضروات

zebra

الحمار الوحشي

hat

قبعة

ruler

مسطرة

unhappy

تعيس

decrease

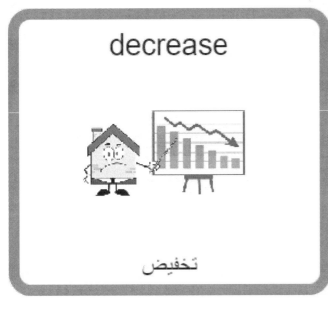

تخفيض

torch

شعلة

snake

ثعبان

fall

خريف

reading

قراءة

nose

أنف

boxing

ملاكمة

backpack

حقيبة ظهر

rob

سلب

smile

ابتسامة

radio

راديو

honey

عسل

chef

طاه

hill

تل

medication

أدوية

collar

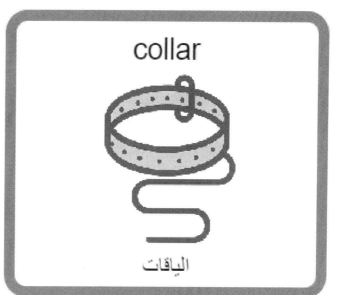

الياقات

bone

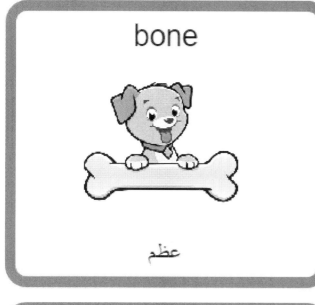

عظم

blood

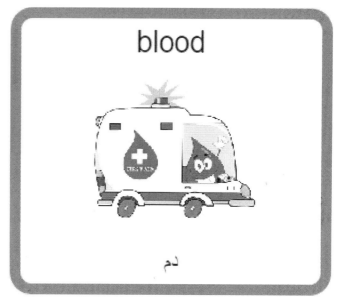

دم

pot

وعاء

love

حب

father

الآب

teacher

مدرس

podium

منصة

bean

فاصوليا

ink

الأحبار

broom

مكنسة

slicing

تشريح

tombstone

تمثال

evil

الشرور

lightbulb

المصباح الكهربائي

oyster

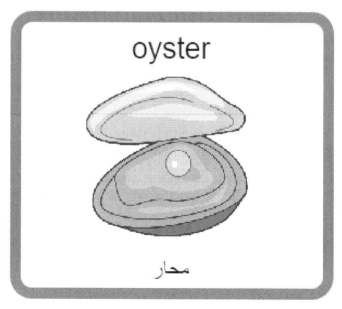

محار

grape

عنب

cowboy

راعي البقَر

hurt

جرح

basket

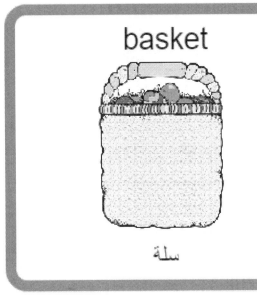

سلة

showering

الاستِحمام

photographer

مصور

impress

اعجاب

lipstick

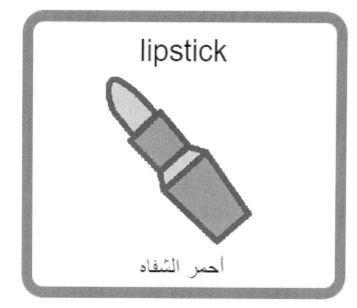

أحمر الشفاه

eight

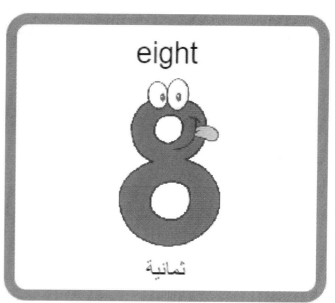

ثمانية

sad

حزين

yogurt

زبادي

throwing

رمي

gifts

الهدايا

massage

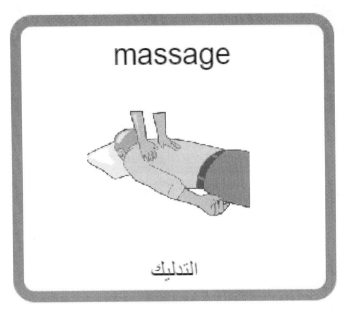

التدليك

sack

أكياس

walk

سير

strawberry

الفراولة

jogging

الركض

tail

ذيل

rooster

ديك

museum

مَتْحف

package

صفقة

diamond

الماس

sandwich

السندويشات

angel

ملاك

math

الرياضيات

swimming

سباحة

flower

زهرة

night

ليل

vase

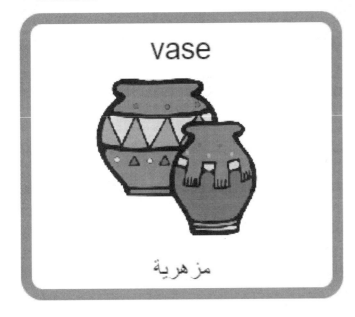

مزهرية

mug

أكواب

kangaroo

كنغر

hot

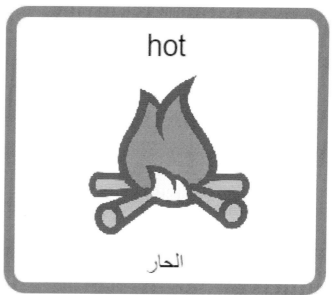

الحار

syringe

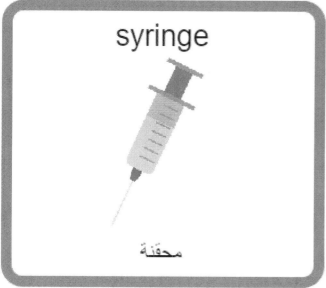

محقنة

princess

أميرة

three

ثلاثة

desk

مكاتب

seeds

بذور

scooter

الدراجات البخارية

him

له

bottle

زجاجة

mole

خلد

puddle

بركة صغيرة

garden

حديقة

bug

بق

coffee

قهوة

sinking

غرق

barrel

برميل

soda

مشروب غازي

presents

هدايا

stop

تَوقَف

sick

مرض

windmill

طاحونة هوائية

alphabet

الأبجدية

donut

الكعك

cage

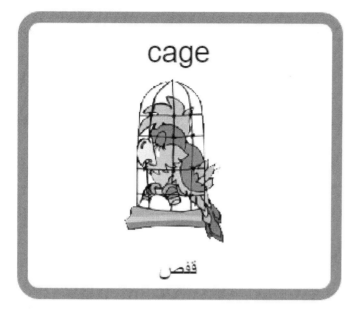

قفص

jump

قفز

stinky

نتن

peg

أوتاد

butcher

جزار

day

يوم

handkerchief

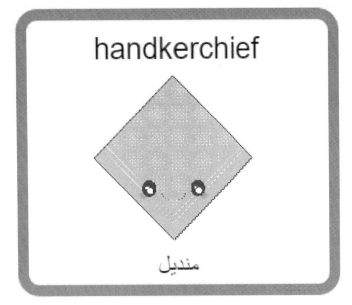

منديل

gasoline

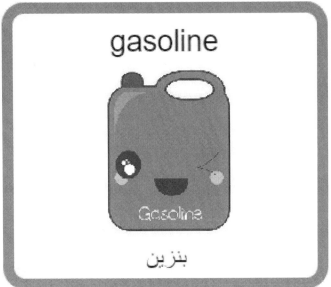

بنزين

pigeon

حمامة

fly

يطير

studying

دراسة عربي

bathtub

حوض الاستحمام

cactus

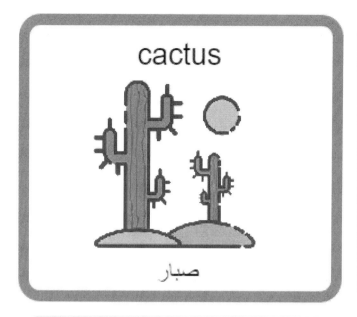

صبار

orange

البرتقالي

enjoy

استمتع

tugging

التجاذبات

bike

دراجة هوائية

driving

القيادة

pig

خنزير

quail

طائر السمان

knight

فارس

tent
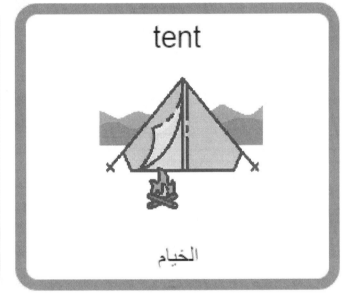
الخيام

bookshelf

رف الكتب

jacket

السترة

igloo

المبني القَبني

fence

سياج

picture

صورة

dig

حفر

airplane

مطار

beard

لحية

ironing

كى الملابس

mop

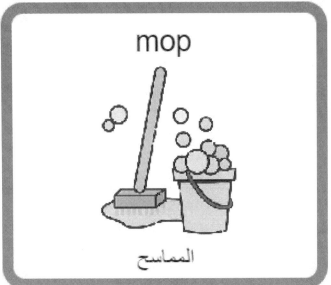

المماسح

pillow

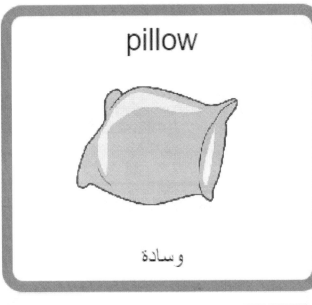

وسادة

skunk

الظربان

team

الفريق

nap

قيلولة

cat

قط

barrow

رابية

bell

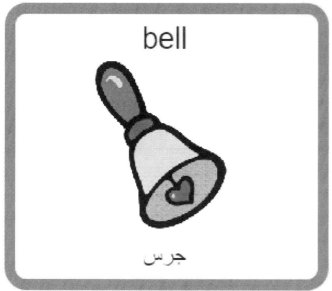

جرس

christmas

عيد الميلاد

teeth

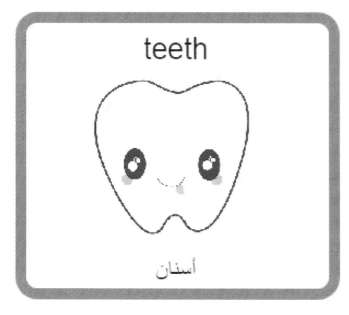

أسنان

lion

أسد

deer

الغزال

chin

ذقن

bored

ضجر

bird

طائر

soup

حساء

sweater

البلوزات

dinner

وجبة عشاء

jug

إبريق

cup

كوب

farm

مزرعة

popsicles

المصاصات

vest

سئرة

fish

سمك

pencil

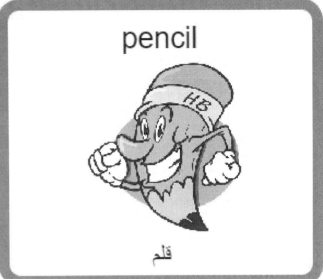

قلم

cheese

جبن

soil

تربة

fishing

صيد السمك

towel

منشفة

song

أغنية

dice

حجر النرد

bite

عضة

onion

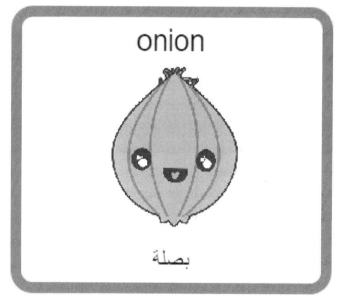

بصلة

four

أربعة

reindeer

الرنة

fire

نار

pineapple

أناناس

milk

حليب

anchor

مرساة

helmet

خوذة

pelican

طائر البجع

castle

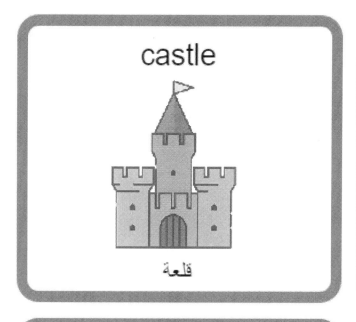

قلعة

dress

فساتين

grapefruit

جريب فروت

soccer

كرة القدم

boots

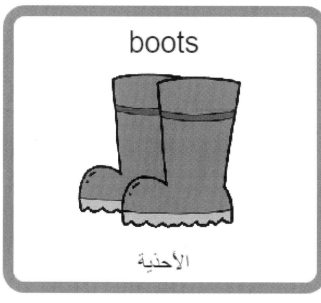

الأحذية

turkey

ديك رومي

number

أعداد

school

مدرسة

delicious

لذيذ

singing

الغناء

lid

الأغطية

family

عائلة

mouth

فم

glue

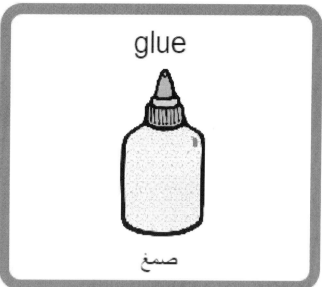

صمغ

musician

موسيقي

candle

الشموع

tire

إطار العجلة

peanut

الفول السوداني

baker

خباز

window

نافذة او شباك

lamp

مصابيح

racket

مضرب تنس

lotus

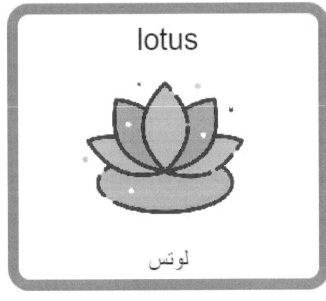

لوتس

rainbow

قوس المطر

trash

قمامة

hammer

شاكوش

maid

عاملة نظافة

earth

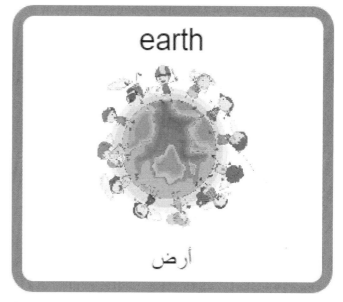

أرض

seven

سبعة

oval

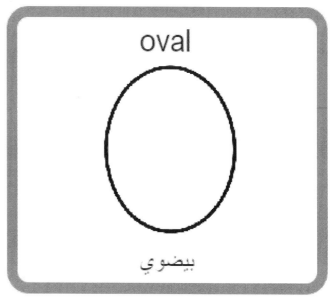

بيضوي

tangerine

يوسفي

kiwi

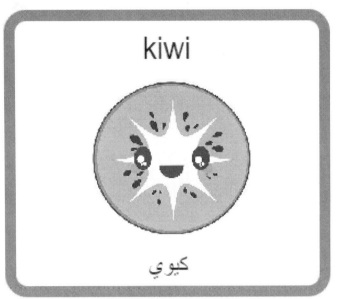

كيوي

teach

علم

penguin

البطريق طائر

house

منزل

shovel

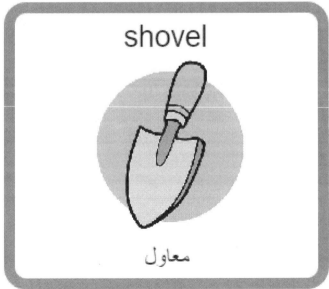

معاول

guitar

غيتار

cute

جذاب

boy

صبي

good

حسن

bouquet

باقة أزهار

skirt

تنورة

sailboat

مركب شراعي

ax

فأس

leader

قادة

nurse

ممرضة

one

واحد

star

نجمة

ostrich

نعامة

cot

سرير نقّال

wag

هز

horse

حصان

mat

الحصير

door

باب

arm

ذراع

shorts

سراويل

briefcase

حقيبة

powerful

قوي

eggplant

باذنجان

computer

أجهزة الكمبيوتر

kitten

قطه صغيره

bus

حافلة

juice

عصير

dust

غبار

map

خرائط

witch

السحرة

cub

الشبل

help

مساعدة

bear

يتّحمل

chalkboard

السبورة

quiet

هادئ

chick

الكتاكيت

wagon

عربة

angry

غاضب

microphone

ميكروفون

tongue

لسان

iguana

الإغوانا

turtle

سلحفاة

wedding

حفل زواج

pulling

سحب

rose

ارتفع

goodbye

وداعا

vaccine

لقاح

train

القطارات

eyes

عين

policeman

الشرطي

meet

يجتَمع

sit

تجلس

ice

جليد

pomegranate

رمان

open

افتَح

nibble

عاب

suitcase

حقيبة سفر

basketball

كرة سلة

wet

مبلل

under

تحت

ring

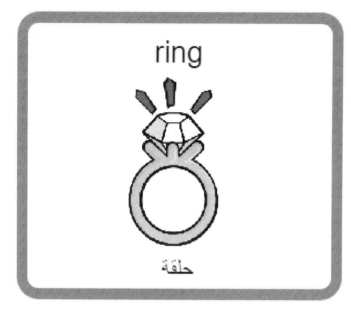

حلقة

joyful

سعيد

boat

قارب

camera

الة تصوير

looking

يبحث

wheat

قمح

brother

شقيق

ant

نملة

brick

قالب طوب

mermaid

حورية البحر

acorn

الجوز

bee

نحلة

raspberry

توت العليق

egg

بيض

yarn

غزل

snail

حلزون

pagoda

معبد

shark

قرش

waiter

النوادل

gorilla

غوريلا

yak

ثور التبيت

wake up

استيقظ

animals

الحيوانات

kite

طائرة ورقية

sleeping

نائم

politician

سياسي

dance

رقص

tame

كبح

monkey

قرد

cucumber

خيار

head

رئيس

ground

أرض

forbid

حرم

run

يركض

six

ستة

red

أحمر

island

جزيرة

win

يفوز

scarf

وشاح

carrot

جزرة

chair

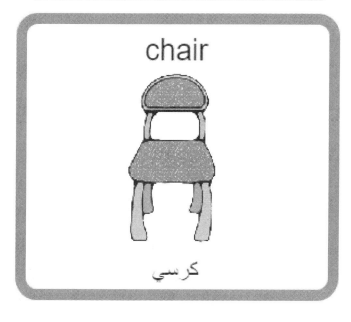

كرسي

umbrella

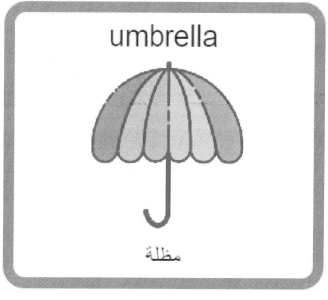

مظلة

mare

فرس

glass

نظارات

drum

طبل

chocolate

شوكولاتة

money

مال

ball

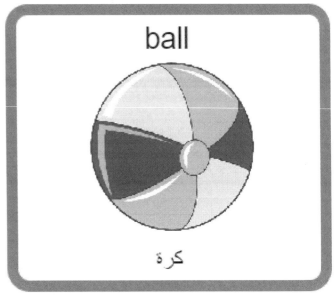

كرة

necklace

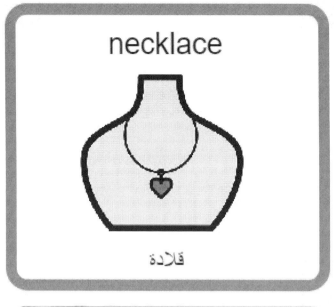

قلادة

cafe

كافيه

street

شارع

carpet

سجادة

eagle

نسر

riding

يركب

monster

مسخ

sketch

رسم

owl

بومة

peas

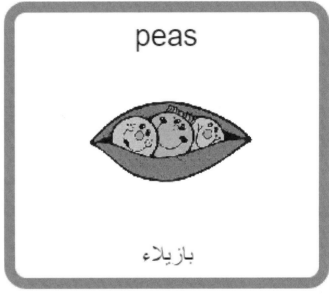

بازيلاء

bed

السرير

hexagon

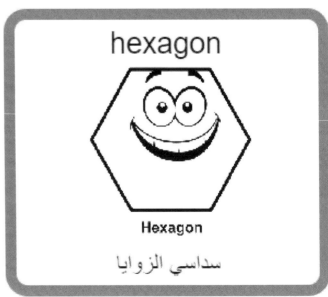

Hexagon

سداسي الزوايا

hedgehog

قنفذ

coat

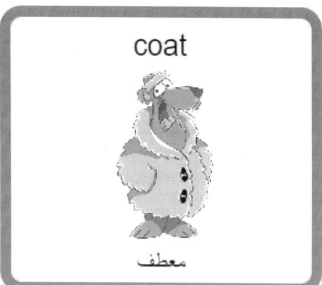

معطف

feeding

تغذية

ice cream

بوظة

shelter

الملاجئ

thunder

صوت الرعد

panda

الباندا

teacup

فنجان شاي

whiskey

ويسكي

turban

عمامة

play

لعب

wood

خشب

zero

صفر

up

فوق

cherry

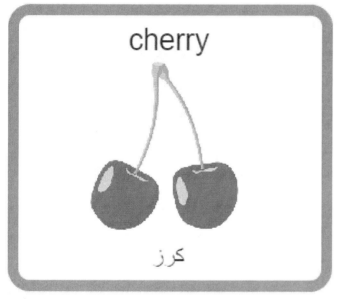

كرز

wreath

إكليل

beach

شاطئ بحر

vulture

نسر

cow

بقرة

muscle

عضلة

groundhog

جرذ الأرض

blender

الخلاط

utensils

أواني

smelling

رائحة

pie

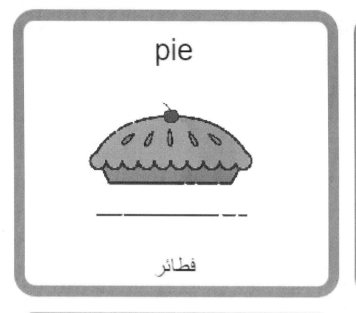

———————

فطائر

scissors

مقص

hospital

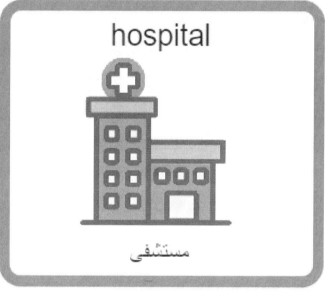

مستشفى

stockings

جوارب

bomb

القنابل

truck

الشاحنات

cake

كيكة

sleepy

نعسان

mother

أم

leaf
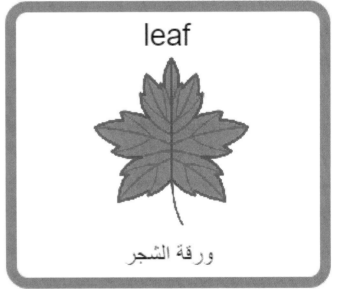
ورقة الشجر

spider

عنكبوت

plum

برقوق

ten

عشرة

bridge

جسر

dad

أب

nine

تسعة

message

رسالة

dolphin

دولفين

pear

إجاص

pen

قلم جاف

artist

فنان

doctor

طبيب

wallet

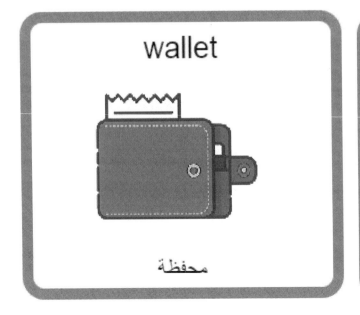

محفظة

magician

ساحر

dumbbells

اجراس صماء

game

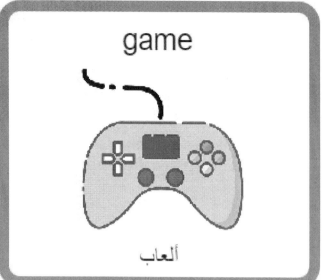

ألعاب

worm

الفيروس المتنقل

nest

عش

shoulder

كتف

loud

بصوت عال

calendar

التَقويم

hotel

الفندق

manager

مدير

face

وجوه

wiping

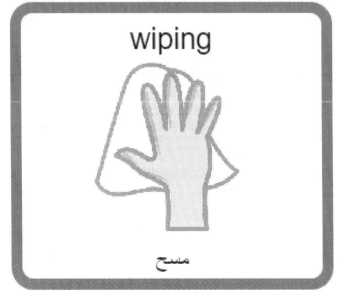

مسح

cheetah

الفهد

name

اسم

butterfly

فراشة

laugh

يضحك

engine
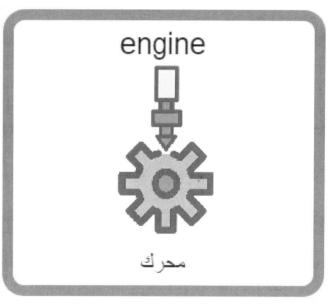
محرك

rabbit

أرنب

earring
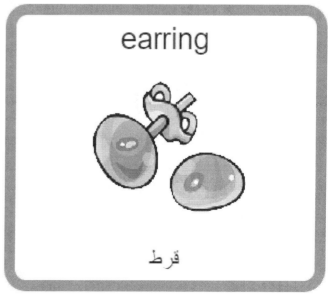
قرط

noodles

المعكرونة

mountains

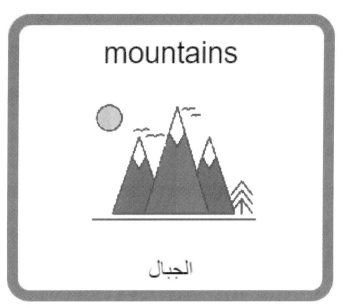

الجبال

pudding

بودنغ

tooth

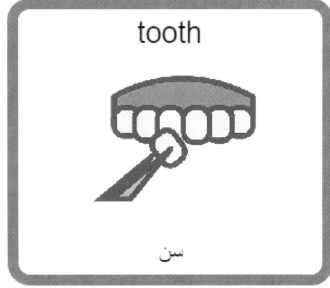

سن

bread

خبز

cop

شرطي

sound

صوت

clean

نظيف

plane

طائرة

stove

موقد

sister

أخت

stylish

أنيق

peach

خوخ

cutter
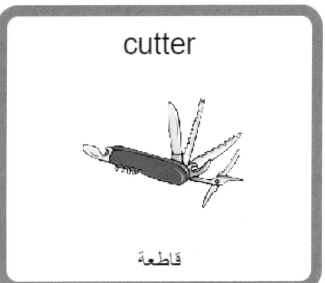
قاطعة

couch

أريكة

stand up

قم

banana

موز

grass

نجيل

strong

قوي

wolf

الذئب

thumb

الابهام

letter

رسالة

respect

احترام

mice

الفئران

wind

ينفخ

baseball

البيسبول

apple

تفاحة

slippers

شباشب

chicken

دجاج

wig

شعر مستعار

ears

آذان

car

سيارة

book

كتاب

lantern

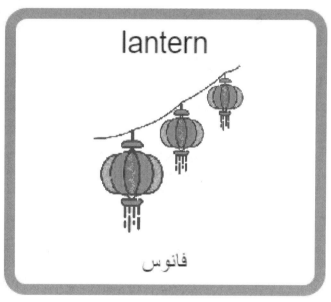

فانوس

serving

خدمة

bowl

عاء

clam

هادئة

mask

قناع

goat

ماعز

hockey

الهوكي

hopping

التنقّل

koala

الكوال دب أسترالي

microscope

مجهر

pacifier

اللهايات

hip

ورك او نتوء

circle

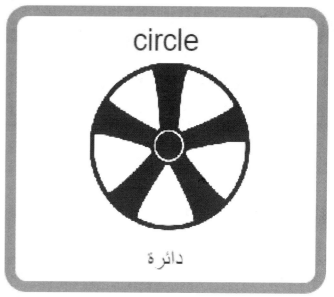

دائرة

violin

كمان

mirror

مرآة

news

أخبار

bag

كيس

toad

العلجوم

eat

تأكل

wash

غسل

toddler

الأطفال الصغار

hide

إخفاء

palm

كف

squirrel

السناجب

pretty

جميلة

shoes

أحذية

clap

صفق

parachute

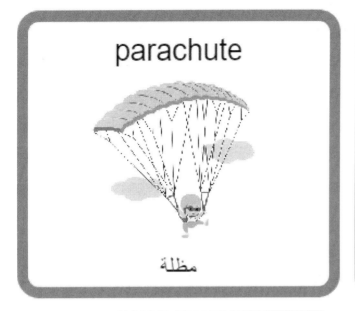

مظلة

giraffe

زرافة

parrot

ببغاء

swan

بجعة

working

عامل

gun

بندقية

unicorn

آحادي القرن حيوان خرافي

camel

جمل

chimney

مدخنة

friend

صديق

bad

سيئة

elbow

كوع

sun

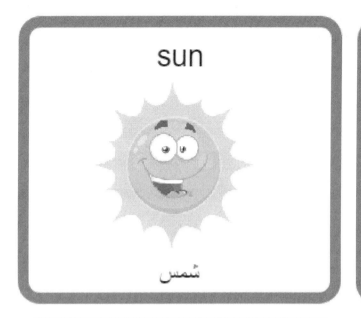

شمس

morning

صباح

shirt

قميص

boar

خنزير ذكر

autumn

الخريف

ham

لحم خنزير

stick

العصي

volcano

بركان

tea

شاي

cry

يبكي

church
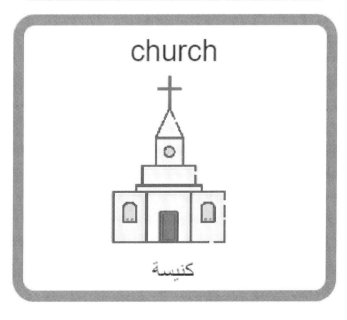
كنيسة

kitchen

مطبخ

question

سؤال

writing

جاري الكتابة

finger

اصبع اليد

man

رجل

bedroom

غرفة نوم

plants

النباتات

snow

ثلج

zipper

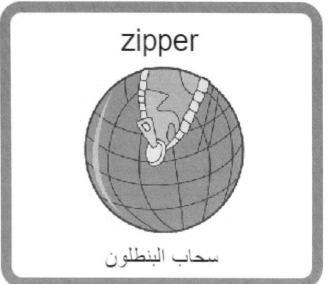

سحاب البنطلون

five

خمسة

compass

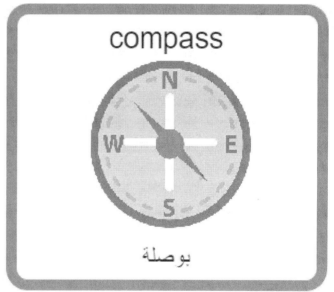

بوصلة

fat

سمين

avocado

أفوكادو

belt

حزام

baby

طفل

dog

الكلب

duck

بطة

dock

الرصيف

kneeling

راكع

golf

جولف

dressing

صلصة

brain

عقل

crayons

أقلام تلوين

girl

فتاة

hit

نجاح

curtain
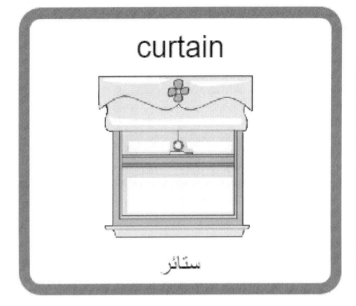
ستائر

queen

ملكة

socks
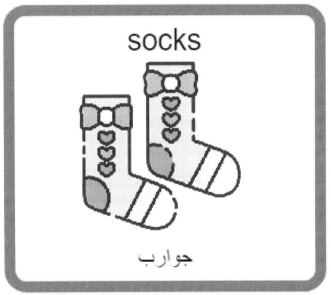
جوارب

rain

تمطر

paintbrush

فرشاة الرسم

broccoli

بروكلي

race

سباق

toy

عروسه لعبه

summer

الصيف

children

الأطفال

two

اثنان

drink

يشرب

celebrate

احتفل

ballon

بالون

tree

شجرة

friendly

ودود

calculator

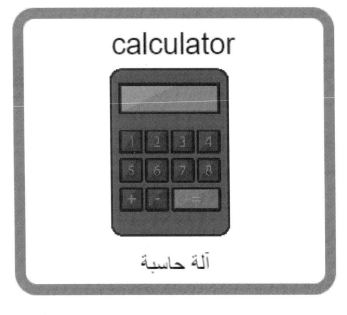

آلة حاسبة

hair

شعر

spatula

ملعقة الصيدلي

sofa

كنبة

corn

حبوب ذرة

pin
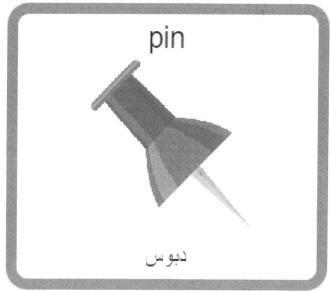
دبوس

lemon

ليمون

mom

أمي

ketchup

كاتشب

steak

شريحة لحم

arrow

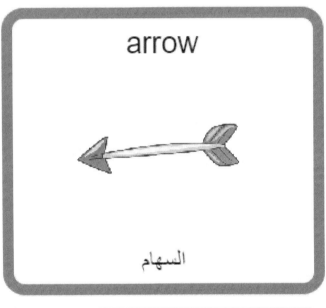

السهام

jeep

سيارات جيب

bib

مريلة

leg

الساقين

telescope

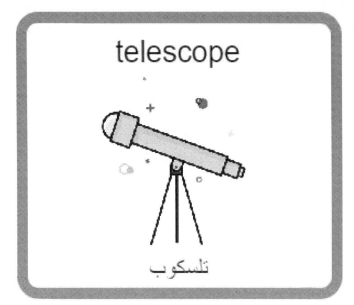

تلسكوب

hug

عناق

mushroom

فطر

quilt

لحاف

climbing

التسلق

hen

دجاجة

puppy

جرو

rocks

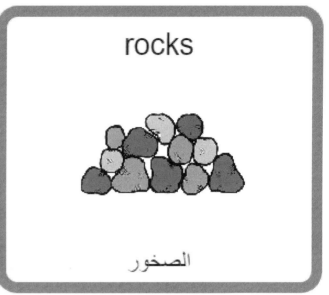

الصخور

big

كبير

kids

أطفال

octopus

أخطبوط

sheep

خروف

knitting

حِياكة

pajamas

لباس نوم

teapot

براد شاى

piano

بيانو

alligator

تمساح إستوائي

prize

جوائز

walrus

حصان البحر

delivery

توصيل

party

حفل

bicycle

دراجة

lizard

سحلية

fitness

اللياقه البدنيه

rake

مجرفة

glove

قفازات

farmer

مزارع

hello

مرحبا

neck

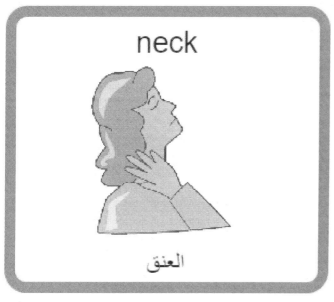

العنق

tomato

طماطم

pizza

بيتزا

clock
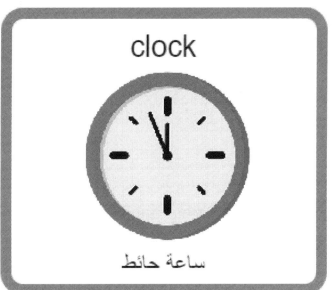
ساعة حائط

body

الجسم

comb
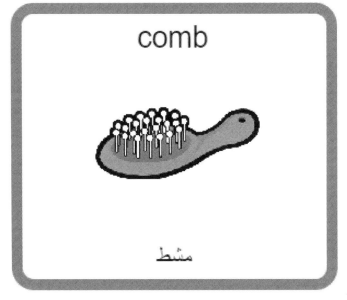
مشط

pirate

القرصان

flag

علم

cookie

بسكويت

oven

فرن

rug

السجاد

meat

لحم

pair

أزواج

mad

مجنون

hand
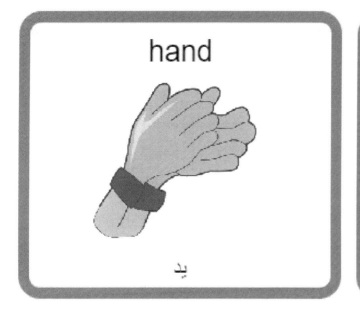
يد

paint

رسم

tray
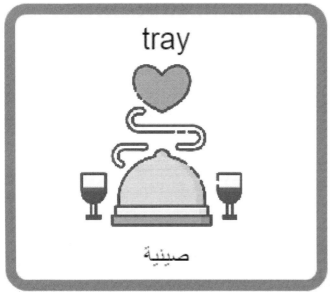
صينية

potato

البطاطس

drawing

رسم

ghost

أشباح

fox

ثعلب

point

نقاط

signature

التوقيع

frog

ضفدع

fin

زعنفة

hippopotamus

فرس نهر

Made in the USA
Middletown, DE
11 December 2024

66636802R00060